GW00375247

THE CANINE FILES

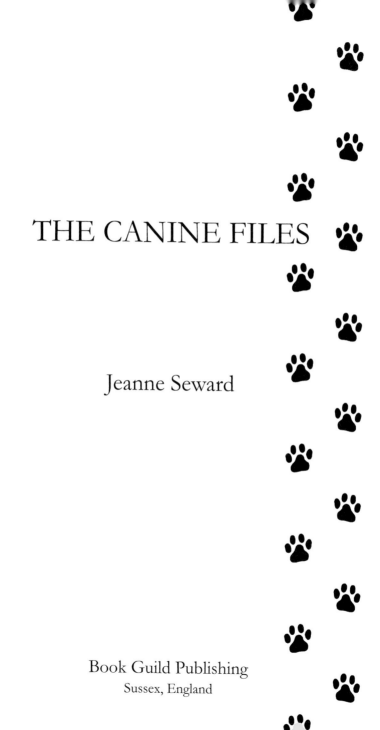

THE CANINE FILES

Jeanne Seward

Book Guild Publishing
Sussex, England

First published in Great Britain in 2009 by
The Book Guild Ltd
Pavilion View
19 New Road
Brighton, BN1 1UF

Typesetting in Garamond

Printed in Great Britain by
CPI Antony Rowe

A catalogue record for this book is available from
The British Library.

ISBN 978 1 84624 338 7

INTRODUCTION

About a week after our golden retriever, Britt, died, my husband, Derek, came home from his regular Sunday pre-lunch drink at the pub and said there was a man there with a litter of ten-week-old puppies which he was giving away. I said I wasn't interested – it was too soon after losing Britt. He said, 'Yes, I know. But why don't you just come and see them. We don't have to have one.' Famous last words! About ten seconds after going into the pub, we were walking out again with the puppy we named Bramble.

We often used to see other dogs in and around Thornbury which were Bramble's double and assumed that they were his brothers and sisters. On one occasion a woman (without a dog) came up to us when we were out with Bramble and asked where we had got him. We told her the story and she said, 'Well, I think someone else who had one of the puppies must have changed their mind and abandoned him in our barn. That's where we found our dog and he is the spitting image of yours!'

Derek had a cousin, Audrey, who lived in Herne Bay, Kent. For some years he had not been in contact with her, then we heard from another relative that she had developed motor neurone disease. We started visiting her, taking Bramble with us. She became very fond of him and after a while it occurred to me that she might find it quite entertaining to get letters 'from Bramble'. This book is a compilation of those letters, followed by ones to Audrey from his successor, Megan.

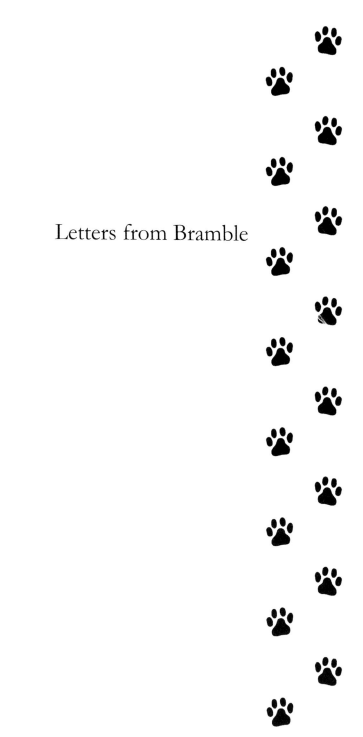

Letters from Bramble

9th May 2001

Dear Audrey,

I have only just discovered how easy it is to use Mum's computer – if I had thought about it sooner I could have started writing to you after our very first meeting. What a waste of time! Never mind, I'll try to make up for it.

Our journey back from Herne Bay was quite exciting at one point. We overtook a van, which was towing a car and in the car's driving seat was a human-being-sized black and white dog, sitting upright with his paws on the steering wheel.* Mum and I were convinced that the dog turned his head and looked at us as we went past, but Dad said we were making it up. We weren't! He did!

I really enjoyed seeing you again (and Tom) and I enjoyed the biscuits you gave me too. I wish we lived closer to Herne Bay – I love going in the water and the sea is a bit more exciting than the little stream I sometimes go in when we are in the Mundy Playing Fields.

I haven't got a great deal to tell you really, so this will only be a short letter, also my paws are getting a bit tired – I'm not used to this typing lark.

Just one thing I must mention, because I know Mum will tell you about it and will almost certainly make it seem that I was being disobedient and taking unnecessary risks. When she took me for my walk this afternoon, we went past the school and onto the big green next to it. Mum was throwing the ball for me, when across the road I saw our post lady. She is lovely and always has treats for the dogs who live on her round. As you may know, we dogs are telepathic and I could tell that she was thinking, 'I wish I could attract Mrs Seward's attention and tell her about the packet I wasn't able to deliver this morning.' So, thinking that she might have the packet with her, I raced across the grass and then across the road (which is quite busy, and I DID LOOK BOTH WAYS) to get to her. She kept me sitting next to her until Mum caught up with me (she's a little bit slow) but the post lady didn't have the packet and Mum will have to go to the Post Office to collect it. Anyway, Mum was really cross with me and said if I was going to behave like that, she would have to keep me on the lead. A bit unfair I think, don't you?

All for now.

With my love,

Bramble

*Author's note: Presumably this was a man dressed up in a dog suit. I feel sure it couldn't have been a toy – much too big.

22nd May 2001

Dear Audrey,

Next week we are going on holiday. We shall be going to our usual place in Wales – 'Come 'ere Igloos' it sounds like but I don't think that's how it's spelt.* Richard will be coming with us, so I shall get plenty of exercise – he throws the ball a *really long way* into the sea and I swim out to get it. This frightens Mum and Dad sometimes and they tell him not to throw it so far, but he is very sensible and ignores them.

I expect you have gathered that I am a very adventurous dog. When I was a puppy I used to squeeze through gaps in the fence and go off for a walk, and Mum would have to come out looking for me. I quite often used to call on a lady who lives near us. She would let me into her house, make a big fuss of me, give me a biscuit, then phone Mum to come and get me. Unfortunately, this didn't last long – they had all the fences renewed so that I couldn't get out. A few months later I managed to dig under the fence, but this time I was a bit stupid and went into the road and got run over. The people in the car – a lady and her two children – knew where I lived and brought me home and Mum and Dad rushed me to the vet's. It turned out that I wasn't badly injured, just a few cuts and bruises, but I was stiff and achy for a couple of weeks. The children who had been in the car were very worried and called to see me several times to make sure I was all right.

I will send you a card next week and when we get back home I will write and tell you about our holiday.

Lots of love,

Bramble   *Author's note:* Cwm-yr-Yglwys.

15th June 2001

Dear Audrey,

Here we are, home again. We had a lovely time and the weather was good, so we were able to get out and about every day.

We often went to Newport Beach, which is quite popular with other dogs and their people. On one particular day there were *nine* other dogs and we all got together and were racing up and down the beach – it was brilliant! We felt like a pack of wolves.

Another place we went to was a castle on the coast, and after we had spent quite a long time looking around it we started back to the car which was parked with several others on the road above the castle. I was well ahead of the others and when I got to the top of the path to the road I noticed that one of the cars had its rear door open. Well, I was hot and tired so I got in and lay down. The people who owned the car didn't mind at all and the lady got in beside me and was patting me and talking to me. Mum, Dad and Richard came rushing up, shouting 'No, Bramble! Not that one!' The people seemed to think it was very funny, and I'm pretty sure it wasn't *me* they were laughing at!

It won't be long now until we come and see you again. I'm really looking forward to it.

Lots of love,

Bramble

22nd June 2001

Dear Audrey,

This morning, when Mum was doing the dusting, she knocked a photograph album onto the floor. It fell open at a picture of me with Gregory, taken several years ago, when Mum and Dad used to look after him when Liz went back to work – and I thought you might like to see it. He was a really nice little boy and I loved playing with him and sharing my chair with him (see other photo). Whenever Mum is talking to anyone about that time, she always says that Gregory was perfect – he was never naughty, never cried, never had a tantrum and always did as he was told. People think she is making this up but I can vouch for the fact that she is at least 99 per cent right.

A couple of days ago we went to see some friends of Mum and Dad, whose garden backs onto a canal, and they have a boat on it. I met them for the first time when I was about six months old. At that time they took us on the boat for a short trip and when we got back I thought that instead of walking down the gangplank I could get ashore more quickly by jumping across onto the bank. It was further than I thought and I fell in. The water was very deep and I went right under and seemed to be down there for AGES but eventually I came up, swam to the bank and climbed out. I didn't know I knew how to swim – I'd never been in the water before. I love the water now and go in whenever I get the chance.

I think I just heard Mum putting my food bowl down, so I will stop, but I'll write again soon.

Love,

Bramble

16th July 2001

Dear Audrey,

I really enjoyed seeing you and Tom again last week, and I'm already looking forward to our next visit. Thank you, Tom, for taking me for a walk in the park (I don't usually go with anyone else, but I knew I could trust you) and thank you, Audrey, for the doggie chocs. I am sorry to say that Mum still gives them to me broken in half, in spite of the excellent example you set her. She's a hard-hearted woman!

I'm sorry I kept scratching myself so much while we were with you – I know it wasn't very polite but I couldn't help it. I'm *still* scratching, I'm afraid, and Mum says she is going to bath me tomorrow. She usually puts lots of old towels down on the floor of the shower and washes me in there. She seems to think it's a brilliant idea but I HATE it. No doubt, once again adding insult to injury, the next day she will complain that the drain from the shower seems to be blocked and say that 'it's probably because of all Bramble's loose hair', conveniently forgetting that she and Dad wash their hair in the shower EVERY WEEK.

We were walking across what Dad calls 'Bramble's Field' the other day when a gull flew overhead, squawking loudly. We all looked up and there, perched at the top of the tree the gull was flying over, was a heron. If the gull hadn't flown over at just that moment we wouldn't have seen it. Mum said she wondered if it was the one that ate all our goldfish – if it was, I'm very grateful. We've got frogs now, instead of fish, and they are much more entertaining.

Lots of love,

9

23rd July 2001

Dear Audrey,

We had some excitement when we went for our walk this morning – well, Mum and Dad got excited – I stayed quite calm. We were walking along a path through a field beyond the Mundy Playing Fields when about ten yards ahead of us a fox walked across. He stopped in the middle of the path and turned and looked at us, then walked on, quite unconcerned! Dad seemed very pleased with me; he patted me and said, 'Well done, Bramble. I was afraid you might chase the fox but you were a good boy.' It was quite nice to get praise, and quite flattering that he must have thought I might actually have caught the fox but I know that foxes have a lot of practice at running away from dogs and he was probably a lot younger than me anyway, so what would be the point?

On our way back we met Keeper and his man. Keeper is a golden Labrador (I don't know why he is called Keeper). He told me when we first met that he was originally trained as a guide dog for the blind, but didn't make the grade (I thought at first that he meant he couldn't go up hills, but it just means he didn't pass the test). He was about eighteen months old when he went to live with his man, David. David and Mum and Dad usually stand and have a chat when we meet, and on this occasion he was telling them the story of when he went with his granddaughter and Keeper to Tenby, in Pembrokeshire, for the day. At lunchtime they stopped at a pub and David fastened Keeper by his lead to a very sturdy bench, which had an umbrella attached to it, just outside the entrance to the pub. David and his granddaughter were just about to order when they heard a commotion and a yelp outside. David rushed out, and both the bench and Keeper had vanished! He ran into the lane beside the pub, and about twenty yards along there was Keeper, still attached to the bench (complete with umbrella) in the middle of the lane, facing a car which was trying to come the other way. He had pulled the bench a total of about thirty yards! It took two men to carry it back to its original position, so perhaps it was because of his immense strength that he wasn't thought suitable as a guide dog.

As usual, they stopped me from going into the stream. I only wanted to cool down but Dad said he'd get wet lifting me into the car. Perhaps when you next speak to him you could casually mention that it might be a good idea when going out with me if he wore something sensible, so that it wouldn't matter if it got wet. You could also mention that the walk is for *my* benefit.

I'll write again soon.

Love,

Bramble

21st August 2001

Dear Audrey,

Our garden gets more like a wildlife park every day. I don't think
I have mentioned it before, but we frequently have field mice
scampering round on the patio, clearing up the remains of the
bird food. There is the occasional hedgehog too and recently we
saw a sparrowhawk, which spent some time sitting on the back of
the garden seat (all the other birds beat a hasty retreat). AND
yesterday there was a *parrot* sitting in one of the trees. Mum saw
it first and called Dad to come and have a look. It was bright
yellow underneath, with blue, red, green and black on its back
and tail and black and white round its neck. It flew onto the fence
and Mum rushed and got some sunflower seeds to throw out for
it. It came down and ate some and then flew off. Mum wondered
whether to tell the RSPCA, but as she had no idea where it had
flown to there didn't seem much point.

Then, of course, there was the fox. It was standing on the
lawn, looking round, so Richard went out and offered it an egg.

The fox took it, went over to the path, dropped it and when it broke lapped it up. Mum got a picture of the fox taking the egg, which I thought you would like to see, so I am enclosing a copy.

There used to be quite a lot of foxes roaming around Thornbury at this time and we sometimes saw them wandering up the road at the front of the house in the evening. As the fox in the garden seemed to enjoy the egg so much, Mum started putting one out on the lawn at the front every night. It was always gone in the morning. One day she was talking to a lady who lives just up the road and the lady said she had been doing some gardening and had found four eggs buried in her flower bed! She was totally mystified by this and Mum just said, 'Really? How extraordinary!' Dad asked Mum why she hadn't told the lady what she had been doing and Mum said, 'I was too embarrassed. I thought she would think I was barmy.'

Mum really missed a golden opportunity last Sunday while we were at the Mundy Playing Fields. Mum and I were walking on ahead of Dad and Richard, on our way back to the car, and we were almost there when we looked back to see how far behind they were. There was no sign of them. We waited and waited, and were just about to go back to see where they had got to when they appeared from round the end of the hedge which borders the tennis courts. Apparently they had been walking along beside the stream and had seen a golf ball in the water. Dad had climbed down the bank and stepped into the water (he was wearing his wellies) to get it. He then started to sink into the mud, and the water was getting closer and closer to the top of his wellies. Richard reached down to grab his arm to pull him out, lost his balance and both of them almost fell into the stream. And we weren't there to see it! AND Mum had the camera with her! I have been gnashing my teeth with frustration ever since.

All for now.

Lots of love,

Bramble

14

17th September 2001

Dear Audrey,

I know Dad has told you, when he has been speaking to you on the phone, that I have been ill recently, and that is why it is such a long time since I wrote to you. I don't quite understand what has been wrong with me – the vet said he thought almost certainly I had had a stroke but I can't make sense of this. During my life I must have been stroked thousands of times but it didn't make me ill. When I first went to the vet with this problem Dad had to carry me in but the second time I went, a few days later, I was able to walk, even if it was a bit lopsidedly. I soon decided I would try going upstairs again but Dad discovered me when I was about six stairs up and now they keep a barrier across the stairs. They really do care about me – it's quite touching.

By the way, Dad has passed your good wishes on to me, and I'm sure that knowing you were thinking of me has helped me to get better.

Mum and Dad have been very good to me while I have been poorly, and I have found that looking a little bit sad always prompts them to give me one of my treats. I find I have to be very careful about letting them know how much I have improved – I am thinking in particular about being able to get up into my chair, which I believe they have told you about. Actually, I have been able to do this for quite a bit longer than they realise, but I have kept quiet about it. Previously, if I wanted to sit in my chair, I would just stand in front of it, with my ears very droopy, tail wagging very slightly, with one paw raised. One of them would immediately rush up to me, give me a hug, and say, 'Oh, poor Bramble, you want to get into your chair!' and they would then help me up. Now, of course, when I try this little ploy, they just say, 'Come on, you old spoofer, you know you can do it!' While there may be an element of truth in this, I'm sure you can understand that remarks like this are extremely hurtful to a sensitive dog like myself.

I am still enjoying my walks and this morning I met four of my friends - a young (slightly scatty) black retriever, two Weimaranas* and dear old Keeper. We haven't seen the fox again.

Talking of wild animals reminds me - apparently the squirrel has visited the garden again. Mum has started putting out nuts in the hope of persuading it to be a regular visitor . . . Not if I have anything to do with it, it won't!

I am looking forward to seeing you again in November.

Lots of love,

Bramble

P.S. I only recently found out what Weimaranas are, so in case you haven't heard of them, they are the same as the one on that television programme called *Watchdog*.

Author's note: Bramble's spelling isn't always perfect!

23rd September, 2001

Dear Audrey,

I had intended to write to you tomorrow, but something happened at lunchtime which changed my mind. Mum and Dad acted very strangely and it was really quite worrying – they had just sat down for lunch, when suddenly they both raised their glasses and said, quite loudly, 'Audrey's toilet!' I couldn't believe my ears – I know that human beings sometimes say funny things before they have a drink, and I've heard 'Cheers!' and 'Here's to you!' and things like that, but . . . 'Audrey's toilet?'* I am hoping that you can make sense of this.

We all had a shock first thing this morning when we went for our walk. When we arrived at the Mundy Playing Fields (we walk alongside the football grounds and through a gate into some other fields), we found that the whole place, including the children's play area, was covered in cows! One of my friends was there with his man, and the man said that yesterday the cows had been on the golf course. I suppose someone had left a gate open somewhere. On the way back some more of my friends had arrived, including Keeper, and we all had a little chat about it. I'm afraid I may have upset one of my friends, a Border collie who looks exactly like Fly, who won the *One Man and His Dog* competition. I said to him, 'Why don't you go and 'round them up?' He glared at me and then said frostily, 'I'm a *Border collie*. We round up *sheep*!'

I got the impression from something Dad said that you were a bit disappointed not to have a paw print on my last letter. I hope this letter makes up for it.

My next vet's appointment is on the 5th October. I think he will be pleased with my progress. Tim (the vet) is very nice, gives me treats and calls me 'Sweetie', but I don't really like going there. The last couple of times I had to have my blood pressure taken and to do this he had to shave some hair off my tail. I looked as if someone had decided to give me one of those idiotic French Poodle haircuts but then changed their mind. There are also other unpleasant things that have to be done which it is probably best not to mention.

The squirrel has not been back, I'm pleased to say. I can't think why Mum wants to encourage him. Last time he was here apparently he dug about four holes in the lawn to bury hazelnuts – I dread to think what would happen if I started burying things in the lawn. It's all terribly unfair; even after a lifetime's devotion I am not allowed to do many of the things I would like to do, but this squirrel (or 'tree-rat' as I like to think of him) comes along and is allowed to tear the garden to pieces. Not only that, but he has his photo taken, and has cashew nuts put out for him. Cashew nuts, I ask you! *I'M* not allowed cashew nuts – oh, no! They might make me fat! I hope that squirrel gets so fat that he falls out of his tree!

All my love,

Bramble

Author's note: By this time Audrey's illness had progressed to the stage where even something like flushing the toilet was impossible for her and she had to ask a visitor or carer to do it. We were able to arrange for a device to be fitted to the toilet so that she just had to move her hand in front of a sensor and it would flush. We were celebrating having heard that this had been done.

27th September 2001

Dear Audrey,

I had not intended to write to you again quite so soon, but I overheard Mum talking about two booklets she had intended to enclose with her last letter. In her usual disorganised way she found she hadn't got an envelope to fit, so it has been left to me to sort things out!

I have got a number of things I want to say, but if I start now I shall miss the post, which is what usually happens with the disorganised person I just mentioned!

I will just tell you that today they have not been using the lower barrier on the stairs and I have been able to go up whenever I want. They still put the top barrier in place when I am upstairs, which is a little bit irritating – they should know by now that I would not attempt anything I wasn't sure I could do. But, as I have said before, I know they have my best interests at heart – bless them.

I will write to you again, at greater length, when I haven't got other people's problems to attend to.

Lots of love, Bramble

29th September 2001

Dear Audrey,

I should have plenty of time to spend on this letter, without any interruptions – Mum, Dad and Richard will be going out at quarter to four this afternoon and not getting back until about ten o'clock. I'd be interested to know what *your* opinion of this behaviour is – leaving a convalescent dog alone for SIX HOURS. I have heard them talking about it, and they do seem a little bit worried, but is that stopping them? Oh, no!

I meant to tell you about a number of things last time I wrote, but didn't have time because of catching the post. First, a very embarrassing episode that occurred when I was being taken for a walk about ten days ago. It was the time we met the Wiemaraners (I spelt it wrongly last time) and as we had not been at close quarters before Dad decided to put me on the lead. The trouble was, he had left it in the car! So he got one of the plastic carrier bags which he always has on him out of his pocket and slipped it through my collar. The indignity of it! I ask you! It was *almost* as bad when Dad was away working recently and had driven off with my lead in the car, so Mum had to improvise. She had to use the carrying strap from Richard's toolbox, which fortunately had clips at the ends, and as it was made of black-and-red webbing it didn't look *too* bad.

When Dad is away we have to walk around the streets – it's too far to the fields – but this isn't as bad as it sounds. One side of the area where we live is bounded by a stream and we are able to walk alongside this. It used to be much better for one of my predecessors, Britt, who was a golden retriever. At that time there were fields (which have now been built on) just the other side of the main road, and there was a pond for her to paddle in. Actually, she wasn't supposed to go in the pond because it was very muddy around the edge and it meant walking her home with her legs and tummy coated in thick mud. Of course, she went in the pond almost every time. Good for her, I say. After all, *the walk is for the dog.* Do you know, a friend of mine told me the other day that his man always says that he likes having a dog because it makes him get some exercise! This is quite the wrong attitude. As I said before: THE WALK IS FOR THE DOG. If I were one of those aristocratic dogs, with a pedigree, I think I might have this as my family motto. I might even have a coat of arms . . .

Sunday, 30th

As it turned out, being on my own for most of the afternoon and evening was a very good thing. First, I usually have my evening meal at six o'clock, but because they were going out I had to have it early, at quarter to four. So, when they got home they were worried that I might feel hungry during the night and gave me FOUR biscuits. Second, it meant that I was able to sleep *undisturbed* for the whole evening. Usually, I feel it is my duty to provide Mum and Dad with something to occupy their minds – after all, what do they do most evenings apart from watch boring television, read or do crosswords? So, although I am always very tired after two long walks and having to check the garden regularly in case we have been invaded by squirrels, I make a point of asking to go out at least once every three-quarters of an hour. They pretend that this annoys them and Dad sometimes says things like, 'I'll wring that ruddy dog's neck if he asks to go out once more,' but I know this is just his little joke and they are both very grateful really. It's the least I can do after they way they have looked after me.

I don't know whether Mum has been reading my mind, or whether she looked at the first part of this letter, but I have discovered that she has been designing me a coat of arms! If she has finished it I will put it at the head of my next letter.

All for now,

lots of love,

Bramble

The Walk is for the Dog

2nd October 2001

Dear Audrey,

I'm afraid you will be getting fed up with letters from me, but I couldn't wait to let you see the coat of arms Mum has designed! She got a book from the library on heraldry to give her some ideas, and I am really pleased – my tail hasn't stopped wagging since she first showed it to me.

The technical description of the Arms is a bit boring, but she insisted I include it, so here goes:

Arms For Bramble, Canis Mongrelus Sable

Shield   A rim Gules with field Tauney and quartered with a cross Or.

         Upper sinister quarter with three bones Purpure, couchant.

- Upper dexter quarter with three bones Purpure couchant.
- Lower sinister quarter with a Canis Laissier Cupra and Argent.
- Lower dexter quarter with Lampus Postis Cupra.
- Shield with two supporters Canis Mongrelus griffins Sable and Argent guardant.
- Scroll borne under the Arms, Gules with Motto Sable on Tauney

There is one small worry about all this – I am deeply suspicious of the words 'Canis Mongrelus'. I can't really believe this is what it sounds like. Mum wouldn't be so unkind; she knows how easily my feelings are hurt.

One last thing. Just because I have my own coat of arms, I don't want you to think that I believe you are in any way inferior to me. I shall continue to treat you as I have always done - as my equal.

Lots of love,

Bramble

The Walk is for the Dog

21st October 2001

Dear Audrey,

I think Mum told you in one of her letters that I was not using the bed she had made out of one of the cushions from my old armchair. Well, this is not my fault! The reason I do not always use it is because Dad will persist in putting my toys onto it, and as one of the toys is a slipper and another is one of those knotted rope things, you can understand that these would not be terribly comfortable to lie on. Fortunately, Mum realised what the trouble was and now she moves the toys onto the floor again. I'm not sure if Dad thought I should move the toys myself if I didn't want them there, but I certainly wasn't going to do that – it would just be the thin end of the wedge, I know. Next thing, I would be expected to clean the floor if I came in with muddy feet, or get my own meals. Actually, getting my own meals wouldn't be such a bad idea, come to think of it – I would have a lot more than I get now, and I would make sure I had more variety; fish for breakfast and chicken for dinner is very nice, but it gets rather boring when you have it day after day.

That reminds me – I did have a bit of lamb at lunchtime today. Mark and his girlfriend came to lunch and she saved me a piece of her lamb cutlet. Wasn't that kind? She has only been here once before, and I was upstairs asleep then, so this was the first time I had seen her. I was very favourably impressed. As soon as she came in she made a big fuss of me, and said, 'Isn't he a love?'

The last two mornings when we have gone for our walk we have arrived at the Mundy Playing Fields at the same time as Keeper, so we have all walked together. I like Keeper very much, but he is only four years old and very boisterous, and a little of his company goes a long way. So this morning, after we had reached the stile into the field, I just stopped. They didn't notice at first that I wasn't with them, and when they saw how far behind I was and clapped their hands for me to come, I just stood there. They soon took the hint and came back to me!

I am hoping that tomorrow they will alter the time of the walk slightly, so that we can go on our own.

Less than two weeks now until we see you again. We are all looking forward to it. I hope the weather is nice so that we can go out together like we did last time.

Love,

Bramble

The Walk is for the Dog

7th November 2001

Dear Audrey,

When I was listening to Mum talking to you about our next visit, I had to smile. I sometimes think that since I became an aristocrat it has gone to her head a bit, because where once she would have said, 'I'll look it up on the big calendar behind the kitchen door', now she says, 'I'll consult my social diary.'

I had hoped to get this letter to you on your birthday, but Mum was hogging the computer for hours yesterday and I didn't get a look-in. I happened to get a glimpse of the photos she sent you and was horrified to see that that pesky squirrel has been back! She hasn't mentioned it in my presence and I think she hopes I don't know about it, but, although my hearing and sight are not what they were, there's nothing wrong with my sense of smell, and even if I hadn't seen the pictures I would have known he'd been in the garden!

After Mum and Dad spoke to you on the phone this morning, Dad went off to get the train to London. He was having lunch with some people he used to work with – they meet every three or four months. Meanwhile, although it is getting close to the time for my afternoon walk, there are no signs that this is going to happen. Admittedly, the rain is coming down in torrents, but she has a perfectly waterproof anorak with a hood, so there is no excuse. She can be very selfish at times.

Love,

The Walk is for the Dog

17th November 2001

Dear Audrey,

It seems a long time since I wrote to you, and as usual this is Mum's fault! For almost a week she was suffering from a bad back, so of course was not using her computer. (She had to miss several walks, too.) This meant that it wasn't switched on, so I couldn't use it either. She hasn't complained much about her back, although it seemed quite painful, and the reason she hasn't complained is that she knows it's her own fault. She carried some very heavy books up the stairs, and instead of being sensible and making two or three trips she did it in one go. Silly woman! Dad was very cross that she hadn't asked him to help her, but he was working in the garden at the time and she didn't want to interrupt him. I think she has learnt her lesson.

I think you have heard about the little Westie puppy we met on a walk the other day. I have never been so embarrassed in my life. They really went 'over the top' and were oohing and aahing, and saying 'Oh, isn't she gorgeous?', 'Isn't she lovely?', 'Oh, bless her', 'Oh, what a little love' and 'You little sweetheart'. It really was quite nauseating – I just walked a little way off, turned away and stood gazing into the distance, trying to ignore it. Of course, it wasn't Jo-Jo's fault that they behaved so soppily; in fact, when we first met I was quite impressed with her. She got a bit overexcited when we touched noses, and started leaping around, waving her front paws in the air, and almost hit me in the eye! But she apologised and called me 'Sir'. I like to see youngsters showing respect.

Did I tell you that my friend Swizzle (he is a Lurcher belonging to David and Joan – David is an old school friend of Dad's) had been in a show near his home a couple of months ago and won the title 'Best Rescue Dog'? This entitled him to go to another show, at Earls Court, which was held on the 4th November. The show is called 'SCRUFFTS'. Unfortunately, he didn't win anything this time, but enjoyed himself very much.

I have at last found out the reason for Mum's rather strange behaviour which started after I became ill. I would be lying down, sleeping peacefully, and when I opened my eyes I would find her leaning over me, staring intently at my chest! This happened many times and I found it extremely unnerving. However, the other day I was lying asleep at the top of the stairs and woke up to find Richard leaning over, staring at me! Mum happened to come upstairs and Richard said to her, 'I couldn't see him breathing. I was just checking that he was still alive!' Well, at least I know now what it was all about, but REALLY! How undiplomatic can you get?

All for now,

Love,

Bramble

The Walk is for the Dog

29th November 2001

Dear Audrey,

It's quite a while since I wrote to you – I hope you didn't think I had forgotten you! Nothing very much of any real interest has happened since my last letter. The condition of my back legs seems to have deteriorated a little in the last few days – when I run I find I have gone back to the slightly sideways motion which I had when I was starting to recover from my stroke – but we have been having some rather damp weather lately and I wonder whether this has affected me. In myself, I feel fine and am still enjoying my walks.

When we are out in the fields I often go off on my own quite a long way, and if Mum and Dad want me to come back they clap their hands (as you know, my hearing is not all that good these days). If I return to them quickly I get a couple of my little biscuit treats. Now, I am telling you this in the *strictest confidence*. I have discovered that if, when I am running away from them, I stop suddenly and look round as if I thought I had heard something and then go back to them, they give me the treats anyway. Sometimes I hear Mum say, 'Oh, bless him, he thought he heard us clap.' I try to resist the temptation to do this *too* often, just two or three times on each walk, because they are not totally stupid and will catch on eventually.

Last night Mum, Dad, Richard and Karen went to the cinema to see *'Harry Potter and the Philosopher's Stone'*, and Mum has been talking about nothing else ever since! When Liz phoned this morning, they were talking about it for at least a quarter of an hour, then she phoned Mark and talked about it again. The Harry Potter film is based on a *children's* book for goodness' sake! Mum is an OAP and Liz and Mark are in their thirties – when are they going to grow up? Even Dad, who is usually extremely sensible, said he thought it was excellent.

Recently, I have been keeping my eyes open for the latest interloper in the garden. Mum and Dad think I don't know about it, but although I am a bit deaf there is nothing wrong with my powers of telepathy and I have a very clear mental picture of this field mouse which has been trespassing on my territory. To use an expression which apparently Mum's mother was fond of – 'If I catch him, I'll show him which way up with care!'
I'll write again soon. Best wishes to Tom.

Love,

Bramble

The Walk is for the Dog

7th December 2001

Dear Audrey,

I am a bit worried about Mum and Dad. They are behaving in the same way that they do every year at about this time. It really is very strange, but I thought that, as you are also a human being, you might know what it's all about. They go out and buy lots of things (most of them aren't even edible!), then, after leaving them lying around in heaps for ages, they suddenly start wrapping them up in coloured paper. It hasn't happened yet, but in previous years this has been followed by a gathering of other members of the family, who share the parcels out between them and rip all the paper off again! If this year is the same as all the others, we shall soon – and I'm sure you will find this hard to believe – have a

TREE in the room. Plants in pots I am used to, but a tree? Oh yes . . . and then of course there will be the crackers, I suppose. I always used to go upstairs out of the way, but this year I don't think it will bother me so much – deafness has its advantages!

Just recently I have not been sleeping all that well. Wednesday night was particularly bad and I had to keep asking Mum and Dad to let me out. I felt very guilty about it, as I know they like to get their sleep, and I didn't actually NEED to go out, if you understand me; I just kept feeling that I must get some air. Fortunately, on Thursday night I slept right through until almost six o'clock. I don't know whether it was because of sleeping so well, but I had a wonderful time on my walk this morning. I was racing about 'like an express train', as Dad puts it. Every now and then, of course, I was going through my 'Oh, did you clap?' routine, and I was so excited with all the running that I didn't take the biscuits in my usual gentle way, and a couple of times I accidentally bit Mum's hand. I'm sure you would have laughed if you had seen it, because each time she gave a little yelp and stood looking at her hand to see if there was any blood! It was absolutely HILARIOUS! Then I slipped when crossing the stream and got soaked – Dad was very funny, pretending to be cross because he would get his coat wet and muddy lifting me into the car. He's got a wonderful sense of humour.

Mum took two more pictures of me several weeks ago, while we were out, and I thought you might like to see them. The one in close-up is a tiny bit blurred but I think it is quite good. The

other one is me 'in goal'.

Still no sign of squirrels or mice in the garden. Mum seems worried that something may have happened to them, but I think they have just got the message that I am not a dog to be trifled with!

The last time I wrote to you I think Dad must have seen my letter heading, because he said to Mum, 'Doesn't that coat of arms look nice? I wouldn't mind one of those myself.' So don't be surprised when you next get a letter from one of them if they have a coat of arms too. I do worry rather that they may be getting above themselves.

That's all my news for now. I'll try to write again soon.

Love,

Bramble

The Walk is for the Dog

16th January 2002

Dear Audrey,

I really have been having a terribly trying time lately. Partly it has been health problems and partly (I'm sorry to say) *neglect* on the part of Mum and Dad. The first mishap was when I went out into the garden and decided to go along the path to the side gate, just in case something needed barking at. There is quite a gap between the path and the fence and it slopes sharply. I missed my footing and fell down the slope, finishing up on my back. I tried to right myself but couldn't, so barked for help – but no one came! I must have been there, my cries getting weaker and weaker, for about two hours, and eventually Dad came out and found me. Mum gave me a cuddle and a biscuit, but I haven't forgiven them

36

yet. Incidentally, if Mum mentions this episode when she writes, she will almost certainly say that I was stuck out there for about three minutes. DON'T BELIEVE HER! IT WAS TWO HOURS AT LEAST!

The second thing happened a couple of days later. I went out into the garden at about half past nine, wandered around for a few minutes, then asked to come in. Do you know what? They had gone shopping and forgotten I was outside! When they got back at about half past ten and let me in they were full of remorse – they could see I was deeply upset that they could do such a thing.

I went for my weekly check-up with the vet this morning. Another humiliating experience. I think either Mum or Dad has told you that I have now got an infection in my . . . er . . . bottom. It was all very embarrassing, and the less said about it the better. Apart from this I am getting on quite well and still enjoying my walks very much.

Not a very cheery letter this time, I'm afraid. Let's hope the next one will be a bit more entertaining!

All my love,

Bramble

The Walk is for the Dog

9th February 2002

Dear Audrey,

I think Mum explained that I had not written to you sooner because I was feeling 'a bit under par'. In fact, I have had a very trying time lately. Last night in particular was dreadful – I simply *could not* get to sleep and had to keep asking to go outside. I got Dad up about three times, and then Mum about four times, after which she decided to try and sleep on the sofa. I suppose this was so that she did not have to keep going up and downstairs, but of course it made me feel terribly guilty, so although she meant well I think this was rather selfish of her. I feel quite a lot better today and enjoyed my walk.

As usual, Mum and Dad were on the lookout for 'their'

robin, so that they could feed it. (Again, although I hesitate to criticise, I would point out that this is supposed to be *my* walk, and not a form of entertainment for *them*.) The robin turned up in his usual place and Mum held out her hand with some food. He flew towards her and for a few seconds hovered over her hand, but then had second thoughts and returned to his twig. From the look on Mum's face while he was hovering, when she thought he was going to sit on her hand, you would have thought she had won the lottery or something! He's only a bird, for goodness' sake. She really is very easily pleased.

On Wednesday our neighbours from Nos. 101 and 102 came in for the evening. As usual I did everything I could to make them welcome, putting my paws on their laps and breathing heavily into their faces, but Mum and Dad didn't appreciate this and kept telling me to go away! I suppose because of my health problems I am more sensitive than usual, but I can't help feeling that they don't really deserve me.

I suppose it's time I had a little walk around the garden again. There are lots of frogs all over the place – I used to enjoy chasing them when I was younger, but now I just creep up behind them, sniff them and make them go leaping away. It's quite fun.

Lots of love,

Bramble

23rd February 2002

Dear Audrey,

Thank you so much for asking Mum to give me an extra chocolate each time she gives me my 'ration' in the afternoon and evening. She gives me my usual three, then always remembers to get out another one and say, 'And this is from Audrey.'

I had quite a lot of trouble at the beginning of my walk today – I just couldn't seem to get my legs working properly. We must have gone about two hundred yards before I could walk normally. I kept collapsing and Dad had to pick me up to get me going again.

When we got to the main field there was great excitement!

40

Mum said, 'Oh, look! Here he comes!' The robin was flying straight for us and landed on a branch just by Mum's shoulder. She held out her hand with some food and, after thinking about it for a little while, he came down. He hovered for a bit, then for a split second he touched her hand with his feet and grabbed a beakful of food, before flying back to his branch. Mum threw the rest of the food on the ground and he went down for it. We started to walk away (with Mum saying over and over, 'He touched my hand! I felt his little claws!') and when we looked back he was following us. Mum offered him some more food, but he waited on his branch until she had thrown it on the ground. I'm very glad we don't see other people too often on our walk – if anyone had seen us this morning it would have been SO EMBARRASSING.

I sometimes think it might be a good thing if we started going to our old field – at least robins wouldn't pester us all the time. But even this would have its drawbacks because the old field has lots of trees and bushes, and Mum and Dad have this game they like to play. They wait until they think I'm not looking, then hide behind a tree or bush. I run about looking for them and when I find them I try to appear very relieved to see them. They say things like, 'You were really worried for a minute, weren't you?' and 'You thought you'd lost us that time, didn't you?' I don't really mind doing this, as it gives them so much pleasure, but it does take up a lot of valuable sniffing time.

I must stop now, as it is almost chocolate time. I will try to write again soon.*

All my love,

Bramble

* *Author's note:* Not to be, unfortunately. Poor Bramble had a relapse and had to be put to sleep on the 15th March – one week before his fifteenth birthday.

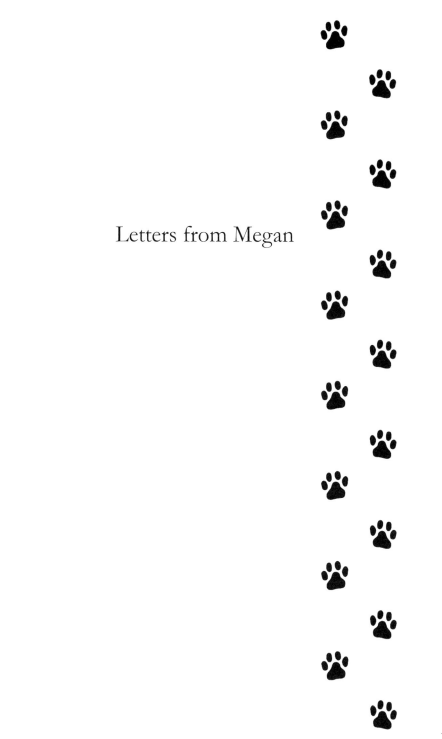

Letters from Megan

A few months after we lost Bramble we decided to get another dog and spent a lot of time visiting the RSPCA dogs' home and also a small privately run place. Eventually, at the private dogs' home, we were introduced to Megan and decided to adopt her. We were told that she was very friendly, loved children and didn't mind cats. To be fair, this is probably what the people who ran the home were told by whoever brought her in, but in fact she dislikes visitors and will keep snapping at their feet. She really didn't (and still doesn't) like children at all and has a pathological hatred of cats! By the time we had discovered her true nature, we had become fond of her, and so we decided to keep her and try to make sure always to be extremely careful when the grandchildren visited (the best-laid plans . . .). Initially, we hoped that in time she would get over her funny ways and we took her to see a behaviourist several times but nothing changed. She couldn't have been nicer with me, Derek and Richard, who at that time was still living at home. She is also fine with our next-door neighbours, Jo and Dennis, who look after her for us occasionally, and we think this is because the first time we left her with them she must have thought, 'Oh, this is my new family now. I'd better watch my step!'

1st February 2003

Dear Audrey,

I had hoped to write to you before this, but it has taken me quite a long time to get the hang of Mum's computer. I was particularly worried about spelling, until Mum pointed out that the computer shows you when you have something spelled wrongly and will put it right for you! Isn't it amazing? Mum says the only problem is that some of the spellings are 'a merry can' – I've no idea what this means, but never mind.

   I have been with my new mum and dad for almost six months now, and I am very happy. They do worry about the way

I behave with visitors and other dogs but this is something I can't help – it is all because of what happened to me in my last home, but I can't bring myself to speak about it yet. I hope you understand.

There are lots of pictures of Mum and Dad's last dog, Bramble, about the house. I am sure I would have got on well with him. When a dog has lived with a family for a long time, other dogs can sense their presence at times, and I have picked up quite a lot about him. Apparently, he was of noble birth and even had a coat of arms!

The food here is wonderful, now that I've got used to it. At first I would only eat bread, because this was all I was given at my last home. But now! This morning I had chicken mixed with little biscuits, with lots of lovely chicken gravy. The trouble is that I get the gravy all round my mouth, but I always go upstairs with Mum after breakfast when she makes the beds and rub my mouth around the sides of one of the beds to clean off. Actually, Mum gets a bit cross about this, and says, 'Why don't you clean your mouth on your own bed?' This is a bit silly really, if she just stopped to think about it. The bed linen on their beds is always being changed, but in the six months I have been here my bedding has only been washed once – can you imagine what it would be like if I cleaned my mouth on it every day?

I hope you like the picture at the top of this letter. It is of my favourite toy, a ball with a string on it, which we take when I go for my walks. They hold the ball by the string when they throw it and it goes a really long way.

That's all for now.

Lots of love,

Megan

12th February 2003

Dear Audrey,

Dad told me that you said you quite enjoyed my letter, so I thought I would write to you again. Actually, quite a lot has happened since I last wrote. I have been in hospital to have an operation! I now have a four-inch gash in my tummy and much smaller gashes on each of my back legs, all held together with stitches. I can't really understand why all this had to be done* but I must say Mum and Dad have been really kind to me while I've been feeling poorly and have given me some lovely meals – the first one I had after coming home was cod and mackerel in tomato sauce, mixed with little biscuits. Delicious!

Talking of food, I feel a bit peeved that they won't let me into the garden after they have put food out for the birds. This is oats, mixed with fat left over from frying. On odd occasions I have managed to sneak out and get some and it is REALLY TASTY! I have to sit in the dining room, watching the greedy little things eating. I don't know if you ever see the *Daily Mail*, but there is a strip cartoon in there called *Fred Bassett*. This dog, Fred, really HATES birds and always chases them, especially if food has been put out for them. He calls them 'little perishers' and I know exactly how he feels.

Dad is getting almost as bad as Mum where birds are concerned. They are both obsessed with trying to get a photo of two robins who come into the garden. All I ever seem to hear these days is, "They're here! Quick! Quick! The camera!" but of course they always fly off. I wish they would just keep still, have their picture taken, and get it over with. Little perishers.

Mum took a picture of me the day after I came home from hospital. She puts my back feet into a pair of ankle socks so that I don't keep worrying at my wounds, but I am finding it hard to cope with the indignity of it all. At least she takes them off before I go out for my walks – I couldn't bear it if any of our neighbours or their dogs saw me.

We have a pond in the garden and the other day when I was out there I noticed that there were funny-looking creatures in the water. They are brownish and about the size of sparrows. I thought at first they were birds that had fallen in, but they haven't got wings so they can't be birds (worse luck!). Mum and Dad don't seem to be in the least worried about them, so I suppose it's all right . . . just as long as they stay in the pond . . . It would be terrifying if they got out, I don't know WHAT I would do!

I had better stop now, as I think it's time for my rest (I get tired very easily since my operation). Unfortunately, before I can lie down in my bed I shall have to work quite hard to make it comfortable. I have a folded-up duvet in it and I like to have one side heaped up to rest my head on. I spend ages getting it just right, and what happens? Mum comes along and says, 'You've messed up your bed again!' Then she gives it a good shake and flattens it out! I never realised that training human beings could be so difficult!

Love,

Megan

Author's note: Megan had to be spayed and while she was under the anaesthetic the vet also removed two dewclaws from her back legs.

25th February 2003

Dear Audrey,

When we were getting ready for our walk on Monday morning, Mum looked for my ball and found that the string had come off, because the knot had come undone. Of course, she blamed me for this and wouldn't spend a few minutes mending it. She decided we would take my old one, which has a great slit in one side and doesn't bounce very well, although the string is still attached. We were about halfway round the field where we walk when I suddenly had a bright idea for getting my own back! Every time they threw the ball, I pretended I hadn't seen where it went and ran the wrong way, so then they had to go and kick about in the tufts of grass, trying to find it! They didn't think it was funny (I did) and in fact Mum referred to me as 'that useless dog!' which I thought was a bit uncalled for.

I had a very unusual meal yesterday evening – in fact, I could hardly believe my eyes when I saw what Mum was putting in my bowl. There was a piece of Quorn and mushroom pie left over from lunch, sprouts and carrots from yesterday's lunch, pasta in tomato sauce, a piece of egg sandwich, some tinned dog food (lamb and rice) and some cheese sauce. I sniffed the bowl very carefully before I started eating but in fact it was delicious. I wouldn't mind having it again. Then something happened that has never happened before – I got a pudding! Sticky toffee pudding with ice cream! Mmmmmmm!

I let Mum read my last letter to you and when she saw that I had called the birds 'little perishers' she said she didn't think this was a very nice thing to say. Well, to keep her happy I'll try to remember not to say it again – but you know what I think of them! Actually, there is ONE good thing about feeding the blackbirds – she always given them a few sultanas, and if I am standing there watching and being very quiet, she gives me some too.* It almost makes it worthwhile having to see the dear little things eating.

Today we went to Tiverton to see Liz, Kevin and the children. Mum and Dad *were very pleased with me* because I only growled once (very quietly) and that was right at the end of the visit when, quite frankly, I was exhausted with all the shouting and rushing about. I had been letting the children throw my ball for me and I was giving it back to them without any fuss.

All my wounds are healing up nicely now and the hair is starting to grow back where I was shaved. This is just as well because if I get tired when I go for my walk, sometimes I stretch out with my tummy on the ground, and if there's been a frost it's a bit chilly!

With all my love,

Megan

*Author's *note:* I have since heard that sultanas can be very bad for dogs, so she doesn't get them any more, although they never seemed to do her any harm.

7th March 2003

Dear Audrey

First of all, Mum has asked me to say she is very sorry that she didn't sign her letter to you yesterday. She says she got 'sidetracked' by having to add the stick-on note and also by having to do a P.S. by hand. Sidetracked my paw! She forgot!

Mum is not quite my favourite person at the moment. Do you know what she did on Wednesday? She lured me up to the bathroom and then bathed me! I was trembling like a leaf with fear but that didn't stop her. To add insult to injury, she hadn't got any proper dog shampoo, so she used Dove shampoo and now I am smelling like a bouquet of flowers. Eeeuugh! As soon as I get the chance while we are out walking I shall find a more appropriate smell to roll in, although I think they know what I have in mind and are keeping a very close eye on me. Oh yes, I almost forgot. To add even MORE insult to injury, after the bathing was finished Mum washed the bath out with disinfectant. Really!

Those things I told you about in the pond that look like birds without wings – apparently they are called frogs. And do you know, they have started crawling out and wandering all over the garden. There was one on the patio the other day and I crept up to it and sniffed it, and it JUMPED! Frightened the life out of me, I can tell you. I try not to spend too much time in the garden now – just rush out and do what is necessary and dash in again.

I always seem to be telling you about things I don't like, and about Mum and Dad getting annoyed with me. So here is some *good* news. Ever since I came to live here I have made a point of watching carefully out of the front window and barking ferociously if anyone walks past. Well, you never know, do you? One of these people might take it into their heads to rush down the path, break in and steal something. But Mum and Dad are so trusting that this thought never occurs to them. They keep saying 'Megan, it's all right. They're just walking past!' Well, I have been trying VERY HARD to control myself and sometimes now I manage to let people go past with just a quiet growl or a very quiet 'Mff, mff'. This makes them very pleased and I get a dog choc for being so good.

Love,

Megan

18th March 2003

Dear Audrey,

I've got some important things to tell you but I must start by saying how much I enjoyed seeing you again. I hope you didn't mind having your face licked so much but I was quite overcome with emotion. And sitting next to you with my chin on your lap while you stroked my head and ears and chest was absolute bliss.

Now, an apology. I know that you and Mum and Dad were very upset because of the way I reacted to Tom.* When you said you wondered if he reminded me of someone I used to see, you can't imagine how close to the truth you were. But the fact is, Tom is not just similar, he is actually THE SAME PERSON. When I lived with my last family, there was a house near us which was the headquarters of a gang of international criminals, who were closely associated with the Mafia, and the man you know as Tom was a frequent visitor there. He didn't look anything like the Tom who visits you (among other things he is a master of disguise and in fact he is now about six inches shorter than he appeared then – he doesn't fool me though) but I cannot emphasise too strongly how dangerous he is. He obviously knew that I recognised him and was afraid I would blow his cover, so he tried to buy my silence with digestive biscuits. My advice is that you should get in touch with the police straight away and tell them all I have told you (you could also add that in Bristol he is known as El Desperanto). As soon as you have contacted the police, lock your door and keep away from the window, as Armed Response Vehicles and men in body armour with sub-machine guns will very quickly surround Donnithorne House.

We went a different way on our walk this morning. I found out afterwards, from something Dad said, that this was because they had seen two mallard ducks sitting near the path we usually take and they didn't want me to chase them. Spoilsports.

Love,

Megan

Author's note: Tom was Audrey's lifelong friend and he lived in the same block of retirement flats. He always came to see us when he knew we were visiting Audrey, and Megan HATED HIM! He invariably brought digestive biscuits with him to give her, in the hope that she might warm to him, but as soon as the biscuits were gone she was ready to try to rip him apart again! We had to keep her on her lead the whole time he was there.

26th March 2003

Dear Audrey,

This letter won't be quite as long as usual because of the size of this notelet. We have run out of A4 paper and Mum forgot to get some more (no comment).

I thought you would like to see the picture of me which was taken during my walk in the Mundy Playing Fields. It is very handy having that stream there because if I get very hot and tired from chasing the ball I lie down in it to cool off, as you see.

Mum has said I should apologise for what I said about You Know Who. She actually read my letter, without asking! Can you believe it? She has explained to me that my suspicions couldn't possibly be true and, while I still have my doubts I feel I should listen to her because for a human being she is quite intelligent. Anyway, I'm sure time will tell, but meanwhile if you haven't already called the police I should put it off for the time being.

I was going to tell you about the brilliant new game I have invented, but I don't think I shall have room, so it will have to wait until next time.

Lots of love,

Megan

27th March 2003

Dear Audrey,

I hope you like the picture at the top of the page. It was taken while I was on Neighbourhood Watch duty. I felt very proud when I first heard that Dad was the local Neighbourhood Watch co-ordinator and made up my mind straight away that I would do all I could to help. Unfortunately, my efforts are not always appreciated and, as I think I have mentioned before, I have to try very hard to control myself. It seems obvious to me that criminals are not going to walk around with a placard round their necks saying 'I am a criminal'; therefore it would be sensible to bark ferociously at EVERYONE, just to be on the safe side. 'Bite first and ask questions afterwards', that's my motto!

Yesterday afternoon I saw a very strange creature in the garden. It was much smaller than a cat, it had a large bushy tail, and it was running along the top of the fence. Mum and Dad noticed I was getting excited about something, and looked out of the window to see what it was. 'Oh, it's the squirrel!' they shouted. It never ceases to amaze me how they react to things like this. Mum immediately started dashing round looking for peanuts, saying, 'Aaah, isn't he sweet?' I'm glad to say that as soon as Mum opened the back door to throw out some peanuts, he scampered off. What is it about small creatures that affects them like this? All they want to do is either *watch* them or *feed* them. They never make the slightest attempt to chase them, which would be the sensible thing to do. I'm sorry, Audrey, but I feel I shall never understand human beings.

I am being allowed to have much more freedom these days. When we are getting ready to go for our walk, I am not put on my lead when we go out of the front door – I am able to have a little walk around the front lawn before getting into the car. Another nice thing is that they sometimes take me with them when they go into the town, although it's a bit annoying when people keep wanting to make a fuss of me. I just stare into the distance and pretend they're not there.

I was going to tell you about the game I have invented, wasn't I? It's brilliant! I get my ball and go to the top of the stairs, put the ball down, then gently nudge it with my nose so that it goes bouncing down … Then I chase it! Sometimes I let Mum join in. We have a little play-fight at the top of the stairs, then she drops the ball down. I race down and grab it and dash back up. Sometimes this goes on for five or ten minutes. I love it.

I'll write again soon.

All my love, *Megan*

61

7th April 2003

Dear Audrey,

Mum has been away for a couple of days and I have been very worried because I was afraid she might not come back again. Dad kept saying to me, 'It's all right, she's only gone to hospital for a little while,' but this didn't really help. Anyway, she's back now, and seemed almost as pleased to see me as I was to see her. As I told you, I went into hospital a little while ago but I don't think it's the same, because when I came home again my tummy had been shaved and I had to wear socks on my back feet. I don't know about Mum's tummy because I haven't seen it, but she certainly isn't wearing socks.

I thought you might like to see some photographs of me searching for frogs in the pond. I don't want to seem boastful, but I am sure you will notice that there is no trace of fear on my face,

although there were lots of them in there. I noticed that there were also an awful lot of little black wriggly things in the water. Apparently, these are baby frogs! If they ALL turn into grown-up frogs, the pond won't be big enough to hold them all and the garden will be about six inches deep with them! I shan't be going out there then, that's for sure!

The other day our neighbours, Jo and Dennis, came in to talk about looking after their house while they are away (they are going to Spain and France with their caravan for THREE MONTHS). When they came in I made a big fuss of them, and when they sat down I got onto each of their laps in turn and licked their faces. Mum and Dad were very pleased with me because the last time they were here I had snapped at them. But later on Mum sent an e-mail to Dennis, which I just *happened* to see, and it upset me very much. At the end, she had put, 'Didn't Megan behave well while you were here? Almost like a normal dog!' I went and sat in my basket and ignored her for the whole evening.

By the way, did you know that the Government has announced an amnesty until the end of the month for people to hand in any illegal guns? Perhaps you could mention this casually in conversation to You Know Who.

All my love,

Megan

15th April 2003

Dear Audrey,

I'm not sure whether Dad told you when he spoke to you on Sunday evening, but on Sunday morning we all (Dad, Mum, Richard, Mark and I) went over to Tiverton because it will be Gregory's birthday soon and we wanted to take his presents to him. Their house isn't *very* big, so you can imagine that with six grown-ups and four children it was quite chaotic, especially as the twins were running about with their dolls' pushchairs. But what I really wanted to tell you was *how good I was*! Several times I was bumped into by a pushchair, but I remained perfectly calm and didn't even THINK about biting anyone. On the journey Mark was sitting in the back seat with Richard and I didn't even try to bite him either. Mum and Dad were pleased about that, although I did howl and whimper a bit on the way there and back and barked every time I saw a lorry.

I think I worried Mum this morning, because she put my breakfast down for me and I only ate about a quarter of it. She thought I must be ill or something, so to put her mind at rest after a little while I ate the rest. Actually, the reason I didn't eat it all straight away was . . . well . . . to tell you the truth, I'm getting a bit tired of fish every morning – and chicken every evening come to that. I know I said that the food was wonderful here, but even gourmet meals get a teensy bit boring when it's exactly the same thing day after day. Not so long ago they used to give me tinned food about every third meal, which was nice (it was really good quality, none of your cheap old stuff) but they found that this was having a rather unfortunate side effect. Even more unfortunately this side effect occurred each evening when I was sitting on Dad's lap, so I don't get tinned food any more. Next time you are talking to Mum or Dad, could you drop a small hint about the value of variety in a dog's diet? I would be grateful.

Oh, I nearly forgot! Something very exciting happened while we were at Tiverton. I was having a look round the house and went upstairs and found a CAT! It raced downstairs, with me only a couple of inches behind it and getting closer all the time, when Mark went and spoiled it all by diving at me and grabbing me round the neck. By the time I had struggled free the cat had gone out of the cat flap. I went back upstairs to see if I could find any more, but no luck. I really LOVE chasing cats, but I don't often have the opportunity. I can't wait to go to Tiverton again!

On Sunday evening Mum put a note out for the milkman for a pint of milk and half a dozen eggs. When she went to get them in on Monday morning, they weren't there, so she phoned the milkman. He had left them, so THEY MUST HAVE BEEN STOLEN! Dad said to me, 'You're always barking at people going past –why didn't you bark when our milk and eggs were being stolen?' I thought this was a bit unfair. After all, it must have happened between about four o'clock and seven o'clock, and even a conscientious guard dog like me has to sleep sometimes.

Lots of love,

Megan

30th April 2003

Dear Audrey,

At last! I have been waiting to write a letter to you for AGES, but for the last couple of weeks the computer has hardly ever been switched on. As you know, I love Mum very much, but I do sometimes wonder if she is quite as bright as she likes people to think. She hasn't been using her computer much lately because she has felt a bit 'under the weather', as you humans say (I'm not sure where else you could ever be, but never mind). But how much time and energy would it have taken for her just to switch it on so that you would at least get a letter from *me*? I do hope that if she has another bout of feeble-itis she will think of this.

My food has been much more varied lately, so I imagine you must have done as I asked and mentioned it to her. Thank you very much.

Our walk the other day was very exciting. I chased a rabbit! I very nearly caught it, too. I was only about six inches behind it, but the little horror disappeared down a hole at the last moment. I couldn't understand Mum and Dad's reaction at all – they were leaping up and down and shouting, 'No, Megan, no! Come here! Leave it!' When I went back to them, they seemed quite cross and said I should leave the 'poor little bunnies' alone. I'll bet if Dad was trying to grow carrots and lettuces in the garden and rabbits came in and ate them all he wouldn't be calling them 'poor little bunnies'!

I expect you remember that my predecessor, Bramble, was a very aristocratic dog, and Mum did some research so that she could design a coat of arms for him. I think she realises that I am a little bit jealous about this, because the other day she was saying to me that it was quite *possible* I might have come from parents of good pedigree. But then she said that if it could be proved that I was a member of the aristocracy, my attitude to other dogs would have to change. You see, I don't like other dogs at all and sometimes I try to attack them if they get too friendly. Mum said that as an aristocrat I would have to be VERY NICE and POLITE to other dogs – she said, 'You've heard of noblesse oblige, haven't you?' Well, actually I hadn't heard of it, but I've got a pretty good idea what it means – it means associating with the hoi polloi when we go for walks, and even *wagging my tail* at these miserable mutts! Well, if that's the price I'd have to pay, I'll stay a mongrel, thank you very much!

On Sunday, Sue (Richard's girlfriend) brought me a bed. It used to belong to her parents' two cats but they didn't use it. The scent of cats was very strong, so as soon as they put the bed down on the floor I got into it straight away and slept in it for about two hours so that my scent would get rid of theirs. For some reason everyone seemed to think this was funny – I think it was because they had put the bed down just inside the front door and I didn't wait for it to be moved to a more sensible place before getting into it. But if a job needs doing, then just get on with it, that's what I say.

Lots of love,

Megan

11th May 2003

Dear Audrey,

Well, that didn't last long. I was really in Mum and Dad's good books for being nice to Mark, but then I spoilt it by attacking the phone man's feet. I try hard, really I do, but something just comes over me. I thought I might have put things right after my walk with Mum on Thursday morning (Dad was going to London, so didn't come with us). I saw another rabbit and with a *supreme* effort of will I stopped myself chasing it. You can imagine my feelings when later on I heard Mum say to Dad, 'There was a rabbit in that little field again this morning, but luckily Megan didn't see it.' It's all so disheartening.

I like to imagine what would happen if Dad *did* grow carrots and a rabbit came and stole one.

This is the rabbit sneaking off with a carrot:

This is Dad, when he sees what is happening:

This is the rabbit, leaving in a hurry:

Tomorrow morning Dad will be changing the posters for the Thornbury Arts Festival, so it will be just me and Mum walking. If I see a rabbit then, I shall stand and stare at it for a long time, so that there can be no doubt that I am *being good!*

I had a horrible experience the other night. I had decided to sleep on my bed up in the bedroom, although mostly I prefer to sleep downstairs. We had all just settled down and Mum had put the light out, when I sensed something creeping towards me. I got up quickly and barked; then, to be on the safe side, I jumped up onto Mum's bed. She put the light on again and when she saw me leaning over the end of the bed, looking down anxiously at the floor, she got up and searched the room to try and find what had frightened me. By this time whatever it was had disappeared, so she put the light out again. Well, I wasn't going to stay there after that! I was just going back downstairs when Richard came in, and he took me into his bedroom and let me spend the rest of the night on his bed. He is so *kind.*

I don't think I've got anything else to tell you this time – apart from scary things lurking in the bedroom, life has been a bit uneventful lately.

Love,

Megan

19th May 2003

Dear Audrey,

I know Mum has mentioned the *Peanuts* cartoons to you in one of her letters; the other day she showed me one about Snoopy writing for a magazine, saying, 'You see, you're not the only dog that writes!' Well, I knew that, even if she didn't.

Mum and Dad went to a lot of trouble on our walk this morning, working out how far I run when they keep throwing the ball. They used some railings with uprights about ten feet apart to measure how far they are able to throw the ball, doubled this to include my run back to them, then multiplied this by the number of throws. All this came to 1,980 yards.

I haven't seen any more monsters in the bedroom lately, but last night when I went into the garden I came across a very strange creature which was even more frightening. I was yelping and barking and Mum came out to see what was the matter. I tried to keep between her and the creature, in case it tried to attack her, but I don't think she appreciated this. She just said, 'Oh, Megan! It's only a hedgehog – it won't hurt you.' Then she took me inside. Well, I didn't know what it was; I've never seen anything like it before. It could have been a monster from outer space for all I knew. I think I was very brave.

Mum and Dad were talking the other day about the time they took me to see a dog behaviourist. I haven't referred to this before because I find it rather embarrassing. They seem to think that there is still room for improvement! Just because I try to protect them when strangers come into the house, and won't put up with any cheek from other dogs! Anyway, Mum said, 'I think what she needs is not so much a behaviourist as a psychiatrist.' I don't know what a psychiatrist is, but they also described this person as 'a shrink'. I find this alarming. I am quite happy as I am – I don't want to finish up looking like a Yorkshire terrier! If they wanted a small dog, why didn't they choose one in the first place? Please could you talk to them about this because I am really worried about it.

It was about a couple of weeks ago that I was taken to the behaviourist.

I had to sit in this room with the three of them for HOURS while they discussed all my faults. When we left, Mum was given several pages of instructions and exercises to do with me. The next day we went through some of the exercises. (I promise you *I am not making this up*.) I had to sit in the middle of the room while Mum walked round me. Then she walked round me again, clapping her hands. Because I had not moved during this I was given a small biscuit. It wasn't obedience that kept me sitting there - it was stunned disbelief. Things got increasingly bizarre, with Mum jumping about then running round me. Then she went out of the room and rang the doorbell . . . Later on I heard her say to Dad, 'How is all that supposed to stop Megan being aggressive?' My thoughts exactly. I have a feeling that she is soon going to get fed up with this (I hope). The advice they got about teaching me to be nice to the children was quite good in some ways. They were told the kids should each be given a bag containing small pieces of raw liver, which they should 'accidentally' drop while walking anywhere near me. That was the good part. But the reason given for doing this is, I feel, an insult to my intelligence - it was supposed to make me think, 'I had better be nice to these children in future, then I will get some more liver.' This wouldn't fool a three-week-old puppy!

All for now. I'm looking forward to seeing you soon.

Love *Megan*

11th July 2003

Dear Audrey,

Something REALLY EXCITING happened this morning. I was upstairs with Mum, keeping her company while she was cleaning the bathroom. When she had finished we started to come downstairs – I glanced through the banisters, and there was a cat in the hall! Needless to say I took off like a rocket and chased it out of the house and across the garden. It went over the fence and I tried to follow, but couldn't quite make it. When I came back in Mum pretended to be a bit put out because I had knocked over a stack of books in the hall, almost toppled the stand with a vase of flowers on it, and sent the doormat and Mum's 'dog-walking' shoes flying across the kitchen. I think it would be worth wrecking the whole house, if necessary, to get rid of a cat and I'm sure she agrees with me really.

I am controlling myself much better now where birds are concerned. I sometimes go out into the garden with Mum when she is feeding the robin or the blackbirds. I sit right next to her and the birds come and eat only about a yard away from her feet – I just watch them, quite calmly.

I don't always feel that I get rewarded properly for my good behaviour. Yesterday they went to Wombourne to see Joan and David and their new dog, Twiglet and when they came home after leaving me for hours and hours and HOURS on my own it hurt me deeply to find that they had the scent of this so-called dog all over them. I say 'so-called' because I happened to see a photograph they had taken of him and well . . . it's not my idea of a dog.

And another thing! Recently we have had a number of people I don't know coming into the house and I have behaved impeccably, not biting them or anything, and what thanks do I get? I hear Mum saying (yet again!) that I am 'almost like a normal dog'. Well, I suppose I have to make allowances for her – she is just a human being after all, poor thing! And she is very good to me in many ways, so perhaps I shouldn't complain.

Oh, dear! What a terribly undiplomatic thing to say! Of course, YOU are a human being too, aren't you? Well, I want you to know that I have always felt about you as Bramble did and consider you to be my equal. Rest assured that I do not look down on you at all.

I discovered the other day, when Dad went next door to feed our neighbours' fish that if I jump over a low part of the fence I can get into their garden. Dad was quite surprised to see me standing next to him! Then later on he went out to post a letter, so I jumped over the fence again, went out of our neighbours' gate, which doesn't close properly, and followed him round to the post box. This surprised him even more! Unfortunately, he always closes the back door now so that I can't follow. Spoilsport.

Lots of love and kisses,

Megan

26th July 2003

Dear Audrey,

It seems such a long time since I wrote to you – I'm afraid I've been in trouble with Mum and Dad again, and part of my punishment has been being banned from using the computer. I think this is *really cruel*, because I enjoy writing to you almost as much as I enjoy going for walks. However, when I tell you the things I did that made them so cross, you may never want to hear from me again!

The first thing happened when the family came from Tiverton to see us. For most of the time I was being *really good*, playing with the children with my ball and letting them tickle my tummy. Then about half an hour before they left, I was getting a bit tired so I got up on Mum's lap. Then Sophie tried to get up on her lap too . . . Then, as they say, I completely lost it. I was overwhelmed with jealousy, and . . . oh dear, I feel so ashamed now . . . but I went for her, and bit her arm. I was immediately pushed out into the garden and had to stay there for the rest of the time they were here. I heard later that Sophie only had a little red mark on her arm, and the skin was not broken; if I had drawn blood I don't think I would ever have been forgiven.

The next thing was when the postman came a day or two later. He had a package and Dad went to the door to get it and I went with him. Usually, now, I am quite calm with people who call. I give them a quick sniff, then I am told to sit down and 'stay' until they've gone, but on this occasion (I think I was still upset from Sunday) I snapped at him. Then the next day a delivery lady came with another parcel, and I snapped at her too. My teeth didn't actually touch either of them, but Mum and Dad were furious with me. I am not allowed to go to the door now when people come. I suppose I shall manage to live all this down eventually. You still like me, don't you, Audrey?

Dad has gone to London today. He left very early, so Richard took me and Mum to the MPF. When Richard throws the ball for me he keeps pretending to throw it one way, and then throws it the other, so I have to run much further. Jolly tiring, I can tell you!

All for now.

Lots of love,

Megan

P.S. I was very sorry to hear that you are in hospital and I hope all the people there are being very nice to you. If any of them haven't been as nice as you would like, I shall be only too happy to bite them for you when we come and see you in September.

24th August 2003

Dear Audrey,

Once again, it is such a long time since I wrote to you – you must think I had forgotten all about you! Nothing could be further from the truth. I have been having a terribly stressful time recently which has left me hardly able to drag myself upstairs, let alone lift my paws to the keyboard. You will see from the picture above what an exhausted state I am in.

The cause of all this is our neighbours. On both sides – Dennis and Jo at 101 and Angela and family at 99 – they have had dogs staying with them. Dennis and Jo's son and daughter-in-law have been on holiday so they have been looking after their two Yorkshire terriers. On the other side, Angela has had friends staying, with their Dalmatian. You can well imagine the burden of responsibility this has placed on me. Hardly an hour has gone past when I have not had to rush to one fence or the other, barking at these interlopers. Actually, the Yorkies aren't so bad; they seem to know their place, but the Dalmatian! The other day when he was being taken for a walk he wrenched the lead out of Angela's daughter's hand and came rushing across the lawn to our front window and started leaping up, snarling and growling, ripping one of Dad's plants out of the ground in the process. Of course, I was going berserk on the inside and knocked an ornament off the window ledge!

The Yorkies have gone home now, but you no sooner get rid of one problem than another crops up – Maurice the Mouse has turned up again! He has started lurking under the lawn mower, which Dad keeps in a corner just to the left of the back door. Mum also keeps a spare supply of bird food there which sometimes gets spilt, so I think this is what attracts him. It isn't just his presence that upsets me – I think I could put up with that – it's Mum and Dad's reaction when they see him. The oohs, aahs and soppy looks really are quite nauseating.

Did Mum tell you about the monster in the bathroom? I was having a little stroll round during the night and as I walked along the landing I happened to look into the bathroom. You remember me telling you about the monster in the bedroom, when I had to leap up onto the bed to get away from it? Well, I think it was the same one, but this time I didn't run away; I stood my ground in the doorway, barking and snarling ferociously, with all my hair on end. Of course, this woke Mum and Dad and they came to see what was the matter, but, as soon as they put the bathroom light on, the monster vanished! You can guess what they said to me, can't you? Yes, that's right. They said, 'Oh, Megan, don't be SO SILLY. There's nothing there!' In spite of this, I shall continue to do all I can to protect them.

That's all for now. See you soon.

With love,

Megan

29th August 2003

Dear Audrey,

As you can see from this picture, I am feeling much more chirpy than I did when I last wrote. All the visiting dogs seem to have gone, I'm glad to say, so it is a bit more peaceful now. Well, it was until breakfast time this morning. Mum suddenly said, 'Oh, look!' and pointed to the window. Just outside, resting his paws on the window frame and peering in at us, was the squirrel. He didn't stay there long when he saw me!

Mum seems to spend all her time lately making cakes. Still, I mustn't complain – she always lets me lick the mixing bowl out. She washes the bowl afterwards with disinfectant, but it's worth putting up with this insult because the cake mixture is yummy.

I was very upset when I discovered that I wouldn't be able to visit you when we come to Herne Bay as you are still in hospital. Perhaps I could wear one of those coats with the letters 'PAT' on it. I believe this stands for 'Pets as Therapy' and apparently some dogs belonging to this society are allowed to visit patients because it does the patients good. I sometimes think human beings are wiser than I give them credit for. Anyway, I'm sure they will be taking you out (in fact, I shall insist on it), so I shall see you then.

Mum and I are still at loggerheads over the fact that I clean my face on the side of her bed after I have had a meal. She doesn't know when she's well off – some dogs would use the furniture in the sitting room.

When I started this letter I thought I had quite a lot to say, but I seem to have run out of topics. Never mind, as soon as anything interesting happens, I will write again.

Lots and lots of love,

Megan

6th September 2003

Dear Audrey,

I would like your opinion on the above picture. Do you think this constitutes animal cruelty? Mum got this stupid idea from reading the PDSA magazine, which has pictures sent in by readers showing their pets doing funny things. I think it's humiliating. Dad said she should send it to the magazine, with the caption (ha ha – *cap*tion): 'Mum said I must wear a hat when it's sunny.'

Perhaps you will let me know what you think when we see you next weekend. I have great faith in your judgement.

Sorry this is such a short letter.

Lots of love,

Megan

15th October 2003

Dear Audrey,

I'm sorry to say that I am still having a very trying time, what with Dalmations, field mice and birds. In the past Mum has sent you pictures of Maurice the Mouse, who comes and cleans up the food that the birds have left. I could put up with that but now he has started bringing his friends! There are AT LEAST two others who are regular visitors, and of course Mum has given them names - Bertram and Timothy. Bertram has a pale patch on his back and Timothy is very, very tiny.   The most annoying thing about them is that although they MUST be able to see me through the dining-room window, they just couldn't care less and aren't in the least scared.

The Dalmatian is still a regular visitor, too. Sometimes he is not on a lead and then he walks all over our lawn, which makes Mum and Dad very cross, but when I bark and growl at him I'm the one that gets told off. Life is so unfair.

Of all the things I have to put up with, I suppose the birds are the least annoying, although I find it rather insulting that – like the mice – they don't seem to care that I am just on the other side of the window (see picture at the top of the page).

Richard came for dinner this evening. It was lovely to see him again – I really miss him.* Mark, Mum and Dad's other son, usually comes on Sunday too, but he has been on holiday in Greece and although he comes home today I think it will be quite late.

It was a beautiful morning when I went for my walk in the MPF but, my goodness, it was cold! When we got to the stream I started to lie down in the water, as I usually do, but I got up again pretty quickly!

Love,

Megan

Author's note: By this time Richard was living with his girlfriend.

8th December 2003

Dear Audrey,

I can't tell you how pleased I am to be writing to you again. You know, don't you, that it hasn't been my fault? Mum and Dad decided that you had 'enough to worry about already' and I was banned from using the computer.* This just goes to show that psychology isn't their strong point.

I thought you might like the enclosed picture, which I'm

afraid isn't very clear. Mum cut it out of the newspaper and copied it for me. Leapfrogging looks like a brilliant game – I wish there were some sheep at the Mundy Playing Fields; I'd love to have a go at it.

Mum decided about ten days ago that I needed a bath. Again! It was HORRIBLE! She put some old towels on the floor of the shower, lifted me in (I had gone limp with fright) and then pulled the shower doors across so that they touched her sides and there was no room for me to escape – she was kneeling on the floor just outside the shower. As usual the shampoo was disgusting and, so far, I haven't been able to find a decent smell to roll in on my walks.

I think I have mentioned before that I am not very keen on other dogs – in fact, I dislike them intensely, especially when they start trying to get friendly. However, for the last few weeks, when Dad takes me for my afternoon walk, we have been meeting a small Border collie – and he's lovely! We run round each other and jump about, and I wish he could come and visit me – we'd have such fun chasing each other round the garden.

Liz, Kevin and the children came to see us a couple of weeks ago. They had been to see Kevin's parents and called in on the way back. They didn't stay very long, just for a cup of tea, but I was very good indeed – I didn't growl once – and played ball with all of them.

Mum did something extremely strange recently. I was in my bed, having my afternoon nap, when I woke up to see Mum walking into the room dressed in Dad's old raincoat with the collar turned up, his cap that he wears when it rains, and an old pair of Richard's heavy black boots. She spoke to me in a very gruff voice and seemed surprised when I ran up to her wagging my tail. I heard her talking to Dad about it later and apparently this was her way of trying to get me used to strange people coming into the house – she thought I wouldn't recognise her! Pathetic!

I think that's all for now. I'll write again soon – I hope you are feeling a bit more settled in your new home now.

Love,

Megan

Author's note: A few weeks prior to this Audrey's health had deteriorated so much that it was decided she should move to a nursing home.

29th December 2003

Dear Audrey,

It's been That Time of Year again! I have been reading through some of Bramble's letters to you and I see he commented on this strange 'Christmas' phenomenon. As he said, why on earth would anyone want to have a tree IN THE HOUSE? But still, Christmas does have its good points. This year I had a present, too. It was from Liz and Kevin – a ball with a bell in it, on a rope. (I didn't tell them I already had one of these, although it hasn't got a bell in it, because I didn't want to hurt their feelings.) I am allowed to play with this ball indoors and I LOVE IT! I hold it by the rope and shake it hard, then I throw it in the air and catch it. It's great fun.

On the subject of balls on ropes, we had a bit of a disaster the other day on my morning walk. I went into the stream, as I usually do, to cool off after all that running, put my ball down in the water, and it got swept away and we never saw it again! I was very fond of that ball. Dad got me a new one, so I still get my regular exercise.

You will have heard that we have had mice in the house – they made the dishwasher break down by chewing through one of the wires (why didn't they get electrocuted?). So you see, I was right all along about those pesky little creatures. Mum put down humane traps for them and then released them in a field. Of course, she still won't let me outside to chase them away . . . AND she still puts food out for them. Some people never learn.

I spent a day with Dennis and Jo a couple of weeks ago while Mum and Dad went to see their friends. I had a lovely time.

Last night, while I was out on the front drive, saying goodbye to Liz, Kevin and the children, Dennis and Jo's son and his wife and little boy arrived to stay with them, and I was able to run across and say hello. I had a look at the little boy and he seemed quite nice, so I didn't bite him.

Love,

Megan

31st December 2003

Dear Audrey,

I forgot to tell you in my last letter about something that happened just after we had had mice in the house. Mum came into the lounge from the kitchen, where she had been preparing the evening meal, and as she walked behind Dad's chair she gave him an affectionate pat on the head. His reaction to this had to be seen to be believed. He leapt to his feet and with a blood-curdling cry, wildly flailed his hands across the top of his head until his hair was all over the place, some of it hanging down like a curtain in front of his face. By this time Mum had started to laugh and he looked round and saw her. 'Oh, it was *you!* I thought a mouse had fallen on my head!' Mum has been laughing about this on and off ever since and getting some very dirty looks from Dad.

This reminds me of something I heard that happened with Bramble once. The grill on the gas cooker wasn't working properly and Mum had sent for the gasman to come and look at it. It was during the summer and he was wearing a short-sleeved shirt. He stood in front of the cooker, doing something with the controls with his right hand, his left arm hanging down at his side. Bramble had come quietly into the kitchen and raised himself up on his hind legs and touched his nose against the gasman's elbow. The man gave a shriek and leapt sideways. When he saw Bramble he said (in a very relieved tone of voice), 'Oh, it's a dog. I thought it was a snake!'

Hope this letter made you laugh too!

Love,

Megan

6th January 2004

Dear Audrey,

Great news !   This morning, when we went for our walk, we met Simon, who is also taken regularly to the Mundy Playing Fields by Benjie, the Border collie. He said, 'I've got a present for you,' and held up the ball which, if you remember, I told you had been lost in the stream. Benjie had found it in the stream much further along, got it out and given it to Simon to give to me. Isn't that marvellous? I'm so glad to get it back.

      I'm pleased Mum didn't tell you any more about what she gave me while she was making the salads to take to Tiverton – I know she would have got it all wrong.   She was cutting things up on the chopping board and I was just sort of hanging about casually near by – in case she offered me anything, or dropped something on the floor. She gave me a few bits of nut, then held something towards me which I didn't recognise and said, 'Here you are, try this – it's a piece of fig.' I misheard her and thought she said 'piece of pig'.   Well, I know that pig is another name for pork, so I was only too glad to accept it! What a shock, though, when I got it in my mouth! Goodness KNOWS what it was, but it certainly wasn't pork! I spat it out and stood looking at it for a little while, then cautiously touched it with my tongue again, but UGH! I stared at it a bit longer, turned and started to walk away. Then I thought, 'Hang on, what if it is some sort of . . . *creature* – it will crawl away and hide, and come out and threaten us when it is bigger.' Well, better safe than sorry I say, so I went back and *rolled* on it for a few minutes! After that I decided it must be dead so I sniffed it again, and actually it didn't smell too bad by that time, so I ate it.

I'm happy to say the house is back to normal again. Mum and Dad have taken down all those silly things they had stuck on the walls and on the banisters, and the tree has gone back in its box. I expect it will all happen again next year, though.

Yesterday Dad decided he was going to clean the bathroom carpet – he said there were dirty patches on it. (I have often noticed that human beings can't bear it when things start to develop a pleasant degree of 'usedness' – they go mad and start cleaning it with foul-smelling soap and things.) He got out the Vax (a sort of wet-and-dry vacuum cleaner), but found that the water wasn't flowing properly. Richard had borrowed it a little while ago, so Dad phoned him to ask if he had had any trouble with it. Richard said he had found that it needed to be raised off the floor a bit to make it work. Dad went back upstairs, put the Vax on the toilet seat, started again on the carpet . . . and pulled the whole contraption off the toilet onto the floor! The carpet was soaked! It took five bath towels to mop it all up. I ran off and got into my bed, so that they wouldn't see me sniggering! Today he tried again, but this time Mum sat in the bath and held the Vax balanced on the side of the bath while Dad worked on the carpet! It is finished now and smells awful – just like I do when I've been shampooed.

Mum and Dad have a friend whose husband is in hospital and she came in for a cup of tea yesterday, after they had given her a lift to the hospital to see him. I let her stroke me and talk to me and I didn't growl once. It wasn't until she was going out of the front door that I even LOOKED at her feet, and I must admit I did give them a tentative little snap, but I don't think she noticed.

That's all my news for now.

Lots of love,

Megan

92

20th January 2004

Dear Audrey,

I have recently discovered that Dad is thinking of giving up being co-ordinator of our Neighbourhood Watch. He sent a notice round telling our members this, but so far no one has volunteered to take his place. What IS he thinking of? The answer is right here in his own house. I would love to do this – and I'm sure I would be pretty good at it! I wouldn't sit at home wringing my paws about all the crime that is going on – I'd be out there running after these crooks and BITING them! Everyone, including the police, would soon notice a difference if I were on the job, I can tell you! I'm afraid I'm going to find it very difficult, though, to convince him that I should be given the responsibility.

The very nice lady whose husband is in hospital, whom I told you about in an earlier letter, has had lunch with us on the last two Sundays. After lunch Mum and Dad took her to see him. Although this lady has never had a dog (she prefers cats – well, no one's perfect), she was very nice to me. While stroking me she was talking to me all the time, telling me how pretty I am and giving me pieces of biscuit. Actually, she reminded me rather of you – I got the same sense of rapport.

Dad was away working in London on Saturday, and again today, on a film called *Colours*. This means that I don't get my usual outing to the Mundy Playing Fields, as it is too far without the car, so Mum has to come with me round the streets. It sounds a bit boring but, in fact, I quite like having the chance to bring myself up to date with what other canines on my 'patch' are up to.

Sometimes, when I am going particularly slowly, Mum says, 'Are you going to sniff *every single blade of grass?*' She doesn't realise that I am just keeping myself informed.

I will write again as soon as I have some more news.*

Lots of love,

Megan

* *Author's note:* Sadly, this was Megan's last letter to Audrey, who died about two weeks later. We were thankful to hear that for her the end was peaceful and quick – sadly, frequently not the case for sufferers from motor neurone disease.